1886-1961

H. D.

SELECTED POEMS

To
my grandchildren
Valentine,
Nicholas,
and
Elizabeth Bryher

H.D.'s settings - (classical)
Sea + mountains - projected sympathetically - abiding places of
  gods, spirits, supernatural beings -
  Seas - wild, terrifying for small boats

Cities - menacing, dangerous, threaten to violate integrity of
  characters and invade privacy of the countryside -
  crowded, clamorous

In Homer the sea is harsh and relentless to provide obstacles
  for heroes to overcome.

H.D. finds in the cold purity of the sea a remedy for the
  ills of social life.

Climbing a mountain is a cleansing from the taint of human
  intercourse and the threat of human love

H. D. *SELECTED POEMS*

GROVE PRESS, INC.   NEW YORK

Sixth Printing

Typography by Peter Bergman (*The Polyglot Press*)
MANUFACTURED IN THE UNITED STATES OF AMERICA

DISTRIBUTED BY RANDOM HOUSE, INC., NEW YORK

CONTENTS

THE HELMSMAN *Charon*

O be swift—
we have always known you wanted us.

Shepherds We fled inland with our flocks, *Central stanzas —*
we pastured them in hollows, *female sexual imagery*
cut off from the wind
and the salt track of the marsh.

We worshipped inland—
we stepped past wood-flowers,
we forgot your tang,
we brushed wood-grass.

We wandered from pine-hills
through oak and scrub-oak tangles,
we broke hyssop and bramble,
we caught flower and new bramble-fruit
in our hair: we laughed
as each branch whipped back,
we tore our feet in half-buried rocks
and knotted roots and acorn-cups.

We forgot—we worshipped, *vaginal*
we parted green from green,
we sought further thickets,
we dipped our ankles
through leaf-mold and earth,
and wood and wood-bank enchanted us—

female — layers of things 7

and the feel of the clefts in the bark,
and the slope between tree and tree—
and a slender path strung field to field
and wood to wood
and hill to hill
and the forest after it.

We forgot for a moment; *the sea?*
tree-resin, tree-bark,
sweat of a torn branch
were sweet to the taste.

We were enchanted with the fields,
the tufts of coarse grass—
in the shorter grass—
we loved all this.

But now, our boat climbs—hesitates—
   drops—
climbs—hesitates—crawls back—
climbs—hesitates—
O, be swift—
we have always known you wanted us.

Sameness

Caressing vowels -

*A new space created by the poet - Not the opposite of
the regular landscape, as in pastoral verse*

*Sea - seems to personify a not unwelcome threat of death -
a harsh kind of peace*

ADONIS

1.

Each of us like you
has died once,
each of us like you
has passed through drift of wood-leaves,
cracked and bent
and tortured and unbent
in the winter-frost,
then burnt into gold points,
lighted afresh,
crisp amber, scales of gold-leaf,
gold turned and re-welded
in the sun-heat;

each of us like you
has died once,
each of us has crossed an old wood-path
and found the winter-leaves
so golden in the sun-fire
that even the live wood-flowers
were dark.

Not the youth loved by Aphrodite.

Oriental hero-god whose death and rebirth symbolized the
decay of winter and the bloom of spring.

One of H.D.'s chaste Olympian heroes who stands for both
purification and rebirth.

2.

Not the gold on the temple-front
where you stand
is as gold as this,
not the gold that fastens your sandal,
nor the gold, reft
through your chiselled locks,
is as gold as this last year's leaf,
not all the gold hammered and wrought
and beaten
on your lover's face,
brow and bare breast
is as golden as this:

each of us like you
has died once,
each of us like you
stands apart, like you
fit to be worshipped.

SEA HEROES

Crash on crash of the sea,
straining to wreck men, sea-boards, continents,
raging against the world, furious,
stay at last, for against your fury
and your mad fight,
the line of heroes stands, god-like:

Akroneos, Oknolos, Elatreus,
helm-of-boat, loosener-of-helm, dweller-by-sea,
Nauteus, sea-man,
Prumneos, stern-of-ship,
Agchialos, sea-girt,
Elatreus, oar-shaft:
lover-of-the-sea, lover-of-the-sea-ebb,
lover-of-the-swift-sea,
Ponteus, Proreus, Ooos:
Anabesneos, one caught between
wave-shock and wave-shock:
Eurualos, broad sea-wrack,
like Ares, man's death,
and Naubolides, best in shape,
of all first in size:
Phaekous, sea's thunderbolt—
ah, crash on crash of great names—
man-tamer, man's help, perfect Laodamos:
and last the sons of great Alkinoos,
Laodamos, Helios and god-like Clytomeos.

Of all nations, of all cities,
of all continents,

she is favoured among the rest,
for she gives men as great as the sea,
valorous to the fight,
to battle against the elements and evil:
greater even than the sea,
they live beyond wrack and death of cities,
and each god-like name spoken
is as a shrine in a godless place.

But to name you,
we reverent are breathless,
weak with pain and old loss,
and exile and despair—
our hearts break but to speak
your name, Oknaleos—
and may we but call you in the feverish wrack
of our storm-strewn beach, Eretmeos,
and our hurt is quiet and our hearts tamed,
as the sea may yet be tamed,
and we vow to float great ships,
named for each hero,
and oar-blades, cut out of mountain-trees,
as such men might have shaped:
Eretmeos and the sea is swept,
baffled by the lordly shape,
Akroneos has pines for his ship's keel;
to love, to mate the sea?
Ah there is Ponteos,
the very deeps roar,
hailing you dear—
they clamour to Ponteos,
and to Proeos
leap, swift to kiss, to curl, to creep,
lover to mistress.

What wave, what love, what foam,
for Ooos who moves swift as the sea?
Ah stay, my heart, the weight
of lovers, of loneliness
drowns me,
alas that their very names
so press to break my heart
with heart-sick weariness,
what would they be,
the very gods,
rearing their mighty length
beside the unharvested sea?

NEVER MORE WILL THE WIND

Never more will the wind
cherish you again,
never more will the rain.

Never more
shall we find you bright
in the snow and wind.

The snow is melted,
the snow is gone,
and you are flown:

Like a bird out of our hand,
like a light out of our heart,
you are gone.

SEA ROSE

Rose, harsh rose,
marred and with stint of petals,
meagre flower, thin,
sparse of leaf,

more precious
than a wet rose,
single on a stem—
you are caught in the drift.

Stunted, with small leaf,
you are flung on the sand,
you are lifted
in the crisp sand
that drives in the wind.

{ Can the spice-rose
{ drip such acrid fragrance
{ hardened in a leaf?

The flowers embody the sea's starkness — are
nurtured to a harsh beauty

H. D.'s sea — less a sun warmed Mediterranean then a chill
expanse of storm and terror.

SEA POPPIES

Amber husk,
fluted with gold,
fruit on the sand,
marked with a rich grain,

treasure,
spilled near the shrub-pines
to bleach on the boulders:

your stalk has caught root
among wet pebbles
and drift flung by the sea
and grated shells
and split conch-shells.

Beautiful, wide-spread,
fire upon leaf,
what meadow yields
so fragrant a leaf
as your bright leaf?

HEAT

O wind, rend open the heat,
cut apart the heat,
rend it to tatters.

Fruit cannot drop
through this thick air—
fruit cannot fall into heat
that presses up and blunts
the points of pears
and rounds the grapes.

Cut the heat—
plough through it,
turning it on either side
of your path.

ORCHARD

I saw the first pear
as it fell—
the honey-seeking, golden-banded,
the yellow swarm
was not more fleet than I,
(spare us from loveliness)
and I fell prostrate,
crying:
you have flayed us
with your blossoms,
spare us the beauty
of fruit-trees.

The honey-seeking
paused not,
the air thundered their song,
and I alone was prostrate.

O rough-hewn
god of the orchard,
I bring an offering—
do you, alone unbeautiful,
son of the god,
spare us from loveliness:

these fallen hazel-nuts,
stripped late of their green sheaths,
grapes, red-purple,
their berries
dripping with wine,
pomegranates already broken,
and shrunken figs
and quinces untouched,
I bring you as offering.

18

1.

Bear me to Dictaeus,
and to the steep slopes;
to the river Erymanthus.

I choose spray of dittany,
cyperum, frail of flower,
buds of myrrh,
all-healing herbs,
close pressed in calathes.

For she lies panting,
drawing sharp breath,
broken with harsh sobs,
she, Hyella,
whom no god pities.

2.

Dryads,
haunting the groves,
nereids
who dwell in wet caves,
for all the white leaves of olive-branch,
and early roses,
and ivy-wreaths, woven gold-berries,
which she once brought to your altars,
bear now ripe fruits from Arcadia,
and Assyrian wine
to shatter her fever.

19

The light of her face falls from its flower,
as a hyacinth,
hidden in a far valley,
perishes upon burnt grass.

Pales,
brings gifts,
bring your Phoenician stuffs,
and do you, fleet-footed nymphs,
bring offerings,
Illyrian iris,
and a branch of shrub,
and frail-headed poppies.

AND PERGAMOS

And Pergamos,
city of the Phrygians,
ancient Troy
will be given up to its fate.
They will mark the stone-battlements
and the circle of them
with a bright stain.
They will cast out the dead—
a sight for Priam's queen to lament,
and her frightened daughters.

And Helen, child of Zeus,
will cry aloud for the mate
she has left in that Phrygian town.

May no child of mine,   *Dissociates self from this*
nor any child of my child   *tale —*
ever fashion such a tale,
as the Phrygians shall murmur,
as they stoop at their distaffs,
whispering with Lydians,
splendid with weight of gold—

"Helen has brought this.
They will tarnish our bright hair.
They will take us as captives
for Helen—born of Zeus,
when he sought Leda with bird-wing
and touched her with bird-throat—
if men speak truth.

"But still we lament our state,
the desert of our wide courts,
even if there is no truth
in the legends cut on ivory,
nor in the poets
nor the songs."

HIPPOLYTUS TEMPORIZES

I worship the greatest first— *loyalty to goddess*
(it were sweet, the couch, *desire for Phaedra*
the brighter ripple of cloth
over the dipped fleece;
the thought: her bones
under the flesh are white
as sand which along a beach
covers but keeps the print
of the crescent shapes beneath;
I thought:
between cloth and fleece,
so her body lies.)

I worship first, the great—
(ah, sweet, your eyes—
what God, invoked in Crete,
gave them the gift to part
as the Sidonian myrtle-flower
suddenly, wide and swart,
then swiftly,
the eye-lids having provoked our hearts—
as suddenly beat and close.)

I worship the feet, flawless,
that haunt the hills—
(ah, sweet, dare I think,
beneath fetter of golden clasp,
of the rhythm, the fall and rise
of yours, carven, slight
beneath straps of gold that keep
their slender beauty caught,

like wings and bodies
of trapped birds.)

I worship the greatest first—
(suddenly into my brain—
the flash of sun on the snow,
the fringe of light and the drift,
the crest and the hill-shadow—
ah, surely now I forget,
ah, splendour, my goddess turns: *Artemis*
or was it the sudden heat,
beneath quivering of molten flesh,
of veins, purple as violets?)

PEAR TREE

Silver dust,
lifted from the earth,
higher than my arms reach,
you have mounted,
O, silver,
higher than my arms reach,
you front us with great mass;

no flower ever opened
so staunch a white leaf,
no flower ever parted silver
from such rare silver;

O, white pear,
your flower-tufts
thick on the branch
bring summer and ripe fruits
in their purple hearts.

OREAD

a nymph of the mountains whose violence is a purification

rhyme

Whirl up, sea—
whirl your pointed pines,
splash your great pines
on our rocks,
hurl your green over us,
cover us with your pools of fir.

Visual, but not a picture.

Cf. C. M. Escher

Verbs convey the surge of waves

Celebrates force and cleansing power of the sea

Greenness in each line— sea, pines, pines, rocks, green, fir

The Oread, a nymph of fertile, green hills and mountains, finds the sea congenial for two reasons: the lifted waves resemble her own green trees — and the image and symbol of green appears in each line

FROM CITRON-BOWER

From citron-bower be her bed,   *a*
cut from branch of tree a-flower, *x*
fashioned for her maidenhead.   *a*

From Lydian apples, sweet of hue, *b*
cut the width of board and lathe, *c*
carve the feet from myrtle-wood. *d*

Let the palings of her bed   *a*
be quince and box-wood overlaid *c*
with the scented bark of yew. *b*

That all the wood in blossoming,
may calm her heart and cool her blood,
for losing of her maidenhood. *d*

Trees mentioned are noted for flowers, fruit, and
pleasant odors. They are both decorative and
symbolically healing.

PALLAS Athene

They said:
she is high and far and blind
in her high pride,
but now that my head is bowed
in sorrow, I find
she is most kind.

Describes people who call goddess blind and scorn speaker for groping after "bloodless things."

We have taken life, they said,
blithely, not groped in a mist
for things that are not—
are, if you will, but bloodless—
why ask happiness of the dead?
and my heart bled.

Flower image shows effect of goddess' presence

Ah, could they know
how violets throw strange fire,
red and purple and gold,
how they glow
gold and purple and red
where her feet tread.

ALONG THE YELLOW SAND

Visual picture

Along the yellow sand
above the rocks,
the laurel-bushes stand.

Against the shimmering heat,
each separate leaf
is bright and cold,
and through the bronze
of shining bark and wood,
run the fine threads of gold.

Here in our wicker-trays,
we bring the first faint blossoming
of fragrant bays:

Lady, their blushes shine
as faint in hue,
as when through petals
of a laurel-rose,
the sun shines through,
and throws a purple shadow
on a marble vase.

(Ah, love,
so her fair breasts will shine
with the faint shadow above.)

THE ISLANDS

1.

What are the islands to me,
what is Greece,
what is Rhodes, Samos, Chios,
what is Paros facing west,
what is Crete?

What is Samothrace,
rising like a ship,
what is Imbros, rending the storm-waves
with its breast?

What is Naxos, Paros, Milos,
what is the circle about Lycia,
what, the Cyclades'
white necklace?

What is Greece—
Sparta, rising like a rock,
Thebes, Athens,
what is Corinth?

What is Euboia
with its island-violets,
what is Euboia, spread with grass,
set with swift shoals,
what is Crete?

What are the islands to me,
what is Greece?

Power of sea.

2.

What can love of land give to me *Female ?*
that you have not—
what do the tall Spartans know,
and gentler Attic folk?

What has Sparta and her women
more than this?

What are the islands to me
if you are lost—
what is Naxos, Tinos, Andros,
and Delos, the clasp
of the white necklace?

3.

What can love of land give to me *giving*
that you have not,
what can love of strife break in me *breaking*
that you have not?

Though Sparta enter Athens,
Thebes wrack Sparta,
each changes as water,
salt, rising to wreak terror
and fall back.

4.

Male reply ?

"What has love of land given to you
that I have not?"

I have questioned Tyrians
where they sat
on the black ships,
weighted with rich stuffs,
I have asked the Greeks
from the white ships,
and Greeks from ships whose hulks
precision of detail lay on the wet sand, scarlet
with great beaks,
I have asked bright Tyrians
and tall Greeks—
"what has love of land given you?"
And they answered—"peace."

32

But beauty is set apart,
beauty is cast by the sea,
a barren rock,
⌈ beauty is set about
⌊ with wrecks of ships,
upon our coast, <u>dea</u>th keeps
the shallows—<u>dea</u>th waits,
clutching toward us
from the deeps.

Beauty is set apart;
the winds that slash its beach,
swirl the coarse sand
upward toward the rocks.

⌈ Beauty is set apart
| from the islands
⌊ and from Greece.

6.   *Sea has possessed the garden
and the speaker*

In my garden,
the winds have beaten
the ripe lilies;
in my garden, the salt
has wilted the first flakes
of young narcissus
and the younger hyacinth,
and the salt has crept
under the leaves of the white hyacinth.

In my garden,
even the wind-flowers lie flat,
broken by the wind at last.

What are the islands to me
if you are lost,
what is Paros to me
if your eyes draw back,
what is Milos
if you take fright of beauty,
terrible, torturous, isolated,
a barren rock?

What is Rhodes, Crete,
what is Paros, facing west,
what, white Imbros?

What are the islands to me
if you hesitate,
what is Greece, if you draw back
from the terror
and cold splendour of song
and its bleak sacrifice?

The sea cleanses the speaker of all human frailties

AT BAIA

I should have thought
in a dream you would have brought
some lovely, perilous thing,
orchids piled in a great sheath,
as who would say (in a dream),
"I send you this,
who left the blue veins
of your throat unkissed."

Why was it that your hands
(that never took mine),
your hands that I could see
drift over the orchid-heads
so carefully,
your hands, so fragile, sure to lift
so gently, the fragile flower-stuff—
ah, ah, how was it

You never sent (in a dream)
the very form, the very scent,
not heavy, not sensuous,
but perilous—perilous—
of orchids, piled in a great sheath,
and folded underneath on a bright scroll,
some word:

"Flower sent to flower;
for white hands, the lesser white,
less lovely of flower-leaf,"

or

"Lover to lover, no kiss,
no touch, but forever and ever this."

35

FRAGMENT 113

"Neither honey nor bee for me."
—Sappho.

[handwritten: Speaker renounces the sweetness of honey and the softness of clinging embraces –]

Not honey,
not the plunder of the bee
from meadow or sand-flower
or mountain-bush,
from winter-flower or shoot,
born of the later heat;
not honey, not the sweet
stain on the lips and teeth;
not honey, not the deep
plunge of soft belly
and the clinging of the gold-edged,
pollen-dusted feet;

Not so—

[handwritten: Power of love which she resists]

though rapture blind my eyes,
and hunger crisp,
dark and inert, my mouth;
not honey, not the south,
not the tall stalk
of red twin-lilies,
nor light branch of fruit-tree,
caught in flexible light branch;

Not honey, not the south;
ah, flower of purple iris,
flower of white,
or of the iris, withering the grass—
for fleck of the sun's fire,
gathers such heat and power,

that shadow-print is light,
cast through the petals
of the yellow iris-flower;

Not iris—old desire—old passion—
old forgetfulness—old pain—
not this, nor any flower,
but if you turn again,
seek strength of arm and throat,
touch as the god;
neglect the lyre-note;
knowing that you shall feel,
about the frame,
no trembling of the string,
but heat, more passionate   *fire - hardness*
of bone and the white shell
and fiery tempered steel.

*Despite her passion, speaker refuses to yield herself
unconditionally. Wooer must agree to her terms,
renounce all claim to soft and coaxing blandishments,
accept her as she chooses to appear, hard and
Athene-like.*

EVADNE

I first tasted under Apollo's lips,
love and love sweetness,
I, Evadne;
my hair is made of crisp violets
or hyacinth which the wind combs back
across some rock shelf;
I, Evadne,
was mate of the god of light.

His hair was crisp to my mouth,
as the flower of the crocus,
across my cheek,
cool as the silver-cress
on Erotos bank;
between my chin and throat,
his mouth slipped over and over.

Still between my arm and shoulder,
I feel the brush of his hair,
and my hands keep the gold they took,
as they wandered over and over,
that great arm-full of yellow flowers.

WHITE WORLD

Visual

The whole white world is ours,
and the world, purple with rose-bays,
bays, bush on bush,
group, thicket, hedge and tree,
dark islands in a sea
of grey-green olive or wild white-olive,
cut with the sudden cypress shafts,
in clusters, two or three,
or with one slender, single cypress-tree.

Slid from the hill,
as crumbling snow-peaks slide,
citron on citron fill
the valley, and delight
waits till our spirits tire
of forest, grove and bush
and purple flower of the laurel-tree.

Yet no one wearies,
joined is each to each
in happiness complete
with bush and flower:
ours is the wind-breath
at the hot noon-hour,
ours is the bee's soft belly, cf. p. 36
and the blush of the rose-petal,
lifted, of the flower.

LOVE THAT I BEAR

Love that I bear
within my heart, O speak;
tell how beneath the serpent-spotted shell,
the cygnets wait,
how the soft owl
opens and flicks with pride,
eye-lids of great bird-eyes,
when underneath its breast,
the owlets shrink and turn.

LAÏS *Greek courtesan – contemporary of Plato*

Let her who walks in Paphos *(Aphrodite)*
take the glass,
let Paphos take the mirror
and the work of frosted fruit,
gold apples set
with silver apple-leaf,
white leaf of silver
wrought with vein of gilt.

Let Paphos lift the mirror,
let her look
into the polished centre of the disk.

Let Paphos take the mirror;
did she press
flowerlet of flame-flower
to the lustrous white
of the white forehead?
did the dark veins beat
a deeper purple
than the wine-deep tint
of the dark flower?

Did she deck black hair
one evening, with the winter-white
flower of the winter-berry,
did she look (reft of her lover)
at a face gone white
under the chaplet
of white virgin-breath?

Laïs, exultant, tyrannizing Greece,
Laïs who kept her lovers in the porch,
lover on lover waiting,
(but to creep
while the robe brushed the threshold
where still sleeps Laïs)
so she creeps, Laïs,
to lay her mirror at the feet
of her who reigns in Paphos.

Laïs has left her mirror
for she sees no longer in its depth,
the Laïs' self
that laughed exultant
tyrannizing Greece.

Laïs has left her mirror,
for she weeps, no longer
finding in its depth
her face, but other
than dark flame and white
feature of perfect marble.

Plato -
translation

Laïs has left her mirror,
(so one wrote)
to her who reigns in Paphos; (Aphrodite)
Laïs who laughed a tyrant over Greece,
Laïs who turned the lovers from her porch,
that swarm for whom now
Laïs has no use;
Laïs is now no lover of the glass,
seeing no more the face as once it was,
wishing to see that face and finding this.

42

HELIODORA Mistress of Meleager, 1⁵c. B.C.

He and I sought together,
over the spattered table,
rhymes and flowers,
gifts for a name. &

He said, among others,
"I will bring"
(and the phrase was just and good,
but not as good as mine,)
"the narcissus that loves the rain." & Meleager's verse

We strove for a name, &
while the light of the lamps burnt thin
and the outer dawn came in,
a ghost, the last at the feast
or the first,
to sit within
with the two that remained &
to quibble in flowers and verse
over a girl's name. &

He said, "the rain-loving,"
I said, "the narcissus, drunk,
drunk with the rain," &
yet I had lost
for he said,
"the rose, the lover's gift,
is loved-of-love,"
he said it,
"loved-of-love;"

I waited, even as he spoke,
to see the room filled with a light,
as when in winter,
the embers catch in a wind
when a room is dank;
so it would be filled, I thought,
our room with a light
when he said,
(and he said it first),
"the rose, the lover's delight,
is loved-of-love,"
but the light was the same.

Then he caught,
seeing the fire in my eyes,
my fire, my fever, perhaps,
for he leaned
with the purple wine
stained on his sleeve,
and said this:
"did you ever think
a girl's mouth,
caught in a kiss,
is a lily that laughs?"

I had not.
I saw it now
as men must see it forever afterwards;
no poet could write again,
"the red-lily,
a girl's laugh caught in a kiss;"
it was his to pour in the vat
from which all poets dip and quaff,
for poets are brothers in this.

So I saw the fire in his eyes,
it was <u>al</u>most my fire,
(he was younger,)
I saw the face so white,
my heart beat,
it was al<u>m</u>ost my phrase;
I said, "surprise the muses,
take them by surprise;
it is late,
rather it is dawn-rise,
those ladies sleep, the nine,
our own king's mistresses."

A name to rhyme,
flowers to bring to a name,
what was one girl faint and shy, *speaker?*
with eyes like the myrtle,
(I said: "her underlids
are rather like myrtle,")
to vie with the nine?

Let him take the name,
he had the rhymes,
"the rose, loved-of-love,
the lily, a mouth that laughs,"
he had the gift,
"the scented crocus,
the purple hyacinth,"
what was one girl to the nine?

He said:
"I will make her a wreath;"
he said:
"I will write it thus:

45

I will bring the lily that laughs,
I will twine
with soft narcissus, the myrtle,
sweet crocus, white violet,
the purple hyacinth, and last,
the rose, loved-of-love,
that these may drip on your hair
the less soft flowers,
may mingle sweet with the sweet
of Heliodora's locks,
myrrh-curled."

(He wrote "myrrh-curled,"
I <u>think</u>, the first.)

I said:
"they sleep, the nine,"
when he shouted swift and passionate:
"*that* for the nine!
above the hills,
the sun is about to wake,
and to-day white violets
shine beside white lilies
adrift on the mountain side;
to-day the narcissus opens
that loves the rain."

I watched him to the door,
catching his robe
as the wine-bowl crashed to the floor,
spilling a few wet lees,
(ah, his "purple hyacinth!")
I saw him out of the door,

I thought:
there will never be a poet
in all the centuries after this,
who will dare write,
after my friend's verse,
"a girl's mouth
is a lily kissed."

HELEN

All Greece hates
the still eyes in the white face,
the lustre as of olives
where she stands,
and the white hands.

All Greece reviles
the wan face when she smiles,
hating it deeper still
when it grows wan and white,
remembering past enchantments
and past ills.

Greece sees, unmoved,
God's daughter, born of love,
the beauty of cool feet
and slenderest knees,
could love indeed the maid,
only if she were laid,
white ash amid funereal cypresses.

AT ITHICA home of Ulysses

Over and back,   Ulysses
the long (waves) crawl
and track the sand with foam;
night darkens and the sea
takes on that desperate tone
of dark that wives put on
when all their love is done.

Over and back,
the tangled (thread) falls slack, Penelope
over and up and on;
over and all is sewn;
now while I bind the end,
I <u>wish</u> some fiery friend Her wish
would sweep, impetuously,
these fingers from the loom.

My weary thoughts
play traitor to my soul,
just as the toil is over;
swift while the woof is whole,
turn now my spirit, swift,
and tear the pattern there,
the flowers so deftly wrought,
the border of sea-blue,
the sea-blue coast of home.

Verse form shows monotony of her existence — regular three stress trimeter. (?)

49

The web was over-fair,
that web of pictures there,
enchantments that I thought
he had, that I had lost;
weaving his happiness
within the stitching-frame,
weaving his fire and fame,
I thought my work was done,
I prayed that only one
of those that I had spurned,
might stoop and conquer this
long waiting with a kiss.

But each time that I see
my work so beautifully
inwoven and would keep
the picture and the whole,
Athene steels my soul,
slanting across my brain,
I see as shafts of rain
his chariot and his shafts,
I see the arrows fall,
I see my lord who moves
like Hector, lord of love,
I see him matched with fair
bright rivals and I see
those lesser rivals flee.

Foreshadowing of
Ulysses' return

LETHE

3   Nor skin nor hide nor fleece   *a*
2   shall cover you,   *b*
3   nor curtain of crimson nor fine   *c*
5   shelter of cedar-wood be over you,   *b*
2 (1)   nor the fir-tree   *d*
1   nor the pine.   *e*

    Nor sight of whin nor gorse   *a*
       nor river-yew,   *b*
nor fragrance of flowering bush,   *c*
nor wailing of reed-bird to waken you,   *b*
       nor of linnet,   *d*
       nor of thrush.   *c*

    Nor word nor touch nor sight   *a*
       of lover, you   *b*
shall long through the night but for this: *c*
the roll of the full tide to cover you   *b*
       without question,   *d*
       without kiss.   *e*

All *b* rimes are identical

Whin = furze
Echoes the rhythm of the tide.
Lethe merges with the great waters of the upper world.

WHERE IS THE NIGHTINGALE

Where is the nightingale,
in what myrrh-wood and dim?
Oh, let the night come black
for we would conjure back
all that enchanted him,
    all that enchanted him.

Where is the b̲i̲r̲d of f̲i̲r̲e,
in what packed hedge of rose?
in what roofed ledge of flower?
no other creature knows
what magic lurks within,
    what magic lurks within.

Bírd, bírd, bírd, bírd we crý,
heár, píty̆ us in paín,
heárts bréak i̯n the súnlight,
heárts bréak i̯n the dáylight raín,
ónly̆ níght héals ăgáin,
    ónly̆ níght héals ăgáin.

O LOVE CEASE

O love cease,
never in porch or corridor
does love come,
never to us,
eternal, tenuous,
who died young,
long ago,
    long ago.

Never to us,
never to us,
did love come,
never to us who strove,
threading the loom,
never to us who sought
dawn and noon,
flame of white flower
whose fire is purer
    than love.

Never to us apart
did love thwart
body and soul and mind
with poisonous dart,   *pain of love*
searing our happiness,
marring content,
    tearing the heart.

Never, O never roam,
naming her sweet,
never invoke,
never entreat
her the dark passion-flower
    treading the foam.

Come
come to Delos,
follow us home,
arise, arise, let us
over the foam,
sing and give answer,
    for life is done.

Never, O never,
wandering from home,
ask of another,
"how did love come?
what is love, sister?
what has he done?"
peace, O my dear ones,
    questioning none.

Soul, soul, O deathless,
soul, soul, O come,
come, come to Delos,
rest and be done,
done with all passion,
    pure and alone.

Come to Delos (death?). Don't seek love.
Love never came to the speaker(s).
Love — painful

54

STARS WHEEL IN PURPLE

Stars wheel in purple, yours is not so rare
as Hesperus, nor yet so great a star
as bright Aldeboran or Sirius,
nor yet the stained and brilliant one of War;

stars turn in purple, glorious to the sight;
yours is not gracious as the Pleiads are
nor as Orion's sapphires, luminous;

yet disenchanted, cold, imperious face,
when all the others blighted, reel and fall,
your star, steel-set, keeps lone and frigid tryst
to freighted ships, baffled in wind and blast.

North star?

THE MYSTERIES REMAIN

The mysteries remain,
I keep the same
cycle of seed-time
and of sun and rain;
Demeter in the grass,
I multiply,
renew and bless
Iacchus in the vine;
I hold the law,
I keep the mysteries true,
the first of these
to name the living, dead;
I am red wine and bread.

I keep the law,
I hold the mysteries true,
I am the vine,
the branches, you
and you.

ERIGE COR TUUM AD ME IN CAELUM

heart

(September 1940)

1.

Lift up your eyes on high,
under the sky—
indeed?
watch planets swerve and lend
lustre to partner-planet,
as they serve
magnetic stress, and turn
subservient to your hands, (God)
your will that guides
majestic cycle of obedient tides?

lift up our eyes to you?
no, God, we stare and stare,
upon a nearer thing
that greets us here,
Death, violent and near.

2.

The alchemy and mystery is this,
no cross to kiss,
but a cross pointing on a compass-face,   compass/cross
east, west, south, north;

the secret of the ages is revealed,
the book un-sealed,
the fisherman entangled in his nets   civilians killed
felled where he waded

for the evening catch,
the house-door
swinging on the broken latch,
the woman with her basket on the quay,
shading her eyes to see,
if the last boat
really is the last,
the house-dog lost,
the little hen escaped,
the precious hay-rick scattered,
and the empty cage,
the book of life is open,
turn and read:

the linnet picking at the wasted seed,
is holy ghost,
the weed,
broken by iron axle,
haemoly - (Milton) is the flower
magicians bartered for.

Feminine space and activity -
the circumference

moly - connected with knowledge and wisdom

CALLYPSO SPEAKS 1938

Callypso

O you clouds,
here is my song;
man is clumsy and evil
a devil.

O you sand,
this is my command,
drown all men in slow breathless suffocation—
then they may understand.

O you winds,
beat his sails flat,
shift a wave sideways
that he suffocate.

O you waves
run counter to his oars,
waft him to blistering shores,
where he may die of thirst.

O you skies
send rain
to wash salt from my eyes,

and witness, all earth and heaven,
it was of my heart-blood
his sails were woven;

witness, river and sea and land;

you, you must hear me—
man is a devil,
man will not understand.

Odysseus (on the sea)

She gave me fresh water in an earth-jar,
strange fruits
to quench thirst,
a golden zither
to work magic on the water;

she gave me wine in a cup
and white wine in a crystal shell;
she gave me water and salt,
wrapped in a palm-leaf,
and palm-dates:

she gave me wool and a pelt of fur,
she gave me a pelt of silver-fox,
and a brown soft skin of a bear,

she gave me an ivory comb for my hair,
she washed brine and mud from my body,
and cool hands
held balm
for a rust-wound;

she gave me water
and fruit in a basket,
and shallow
baskets of pulse and grain, and a ball
of hemp

pulse — seeds of leguminous plants such as beans, peas, lentils

for mending the sail;

she gave me a willow-basket
for letting into the shallows
for eels;

she gave me peace in her cave.

Callypso (from land)

He has gone,
he has forgotten;
he took my lute and my shell of crystal—
he never looked back—

Odysseus (on the sea)

She gave me a wooden flute
and a mantle,
she wove this wool—

Callypso (from land)

For man is a brute and a fool.

Traditional Callypso is grief-stricken. H.D.'s is
outraged.

BIRD OF THE AIR

(From the *Ion* of Euripedes.)

Ion: Bird
of the air,
O, bright legate,
wing back,
back,
I say,
to Parnassus;
off, off the cornice,
that bright peak,
that gold ledge
is no perch for your feet;
O, eagle,
back,
back
where you hold court,
commanding all birds
with your sharp beak;

bird
of the lake,
O, fair,
fairest
of birds
and beloved of king Phoibos,
O, swan
of the white wing,
the red feet,
wing back,

back, I say,
to lake Delos;
O, voice that is tuned
to his harp-note,
O, throat
must I pierce you
with my dart?
be off,
O, my swan
lest your blood drip
red death
on this beautiful pavement;

bird
of the wood,
must you have gold?
these gifts
were not set here
for bird-nests;
bird,
bird
of the woods,
seek your forests
by the isthmus
or near
river Alpheus,
my dart
warns you,
here it is dangerous
for you
and your fledgelings;
O, be off;

my arrow has no choice,
nor I;
I am the god's
and I obey;

but
O, you birds
of lake and forest,
you swan,
you wood-bird
and you legate
of Zeus,
even as I string my bow,
I pray,
be off,
be off,
for I must slay
intruders here
within the precinct;

back to Parnassus
and your nests,
back,
back,
O, God's majestic legate,
back,
back,
O, swan,
my Lord's delight,
back,
back
O, little birds who sing;

for this,
O, this, I would not kill,
your song
that tells to men,
God's will.

THE MOON IN YOUR HANDS

If you take the moon in your hands
and turn it round
(heavy, slightly tarnished platter)
you're there;

if you pull dry sea-weed from the sand
and turn it round
and wonder at the underside's bright amber,
your eyes

look out as they did here,
(you don't remember)
when my soul turned round,

perceiving the other-side of everything,
mullein-leaf, dogwood-leaf, moth-wing
and dandelion-seed under the ground.

FAIR THE THREAD

Fall the deep curtains,
delicate the weave,
fair the thread:

clear the colours,
apple-leaf green,
ox-heart blood-red:

rare the texture,
woven from wild ram,
sea-bred horned sheep:

the stallion and his mare,
unbridled, with arrow-pattern,
are worked on

the blue cloth
before the door
of religion and inspiration:

the scorpion, snake and hawk
are gold-patterned
as on a king's pall.

GEORGIUS SANCTUS

(For William Morris, 1834-1896)

Enemy of earth's desolation,
Husbandman, guardian of peace,
Raise your gónfalon over us,
Georgius Sanctus,

Illuminated Book of Hours,
Thrones, Powers, and Dominions,
Chevalier of the Golden Fleece,
Georgius Sanctus,

Marshall of Knighthood,
Sceptre of fleur-de-lys,
Holy champion of beauty,
Georgius Sanctus,

Protector of shrine and sanctuary,
Soldier-Saint and Crusader,
Herald of Chivalry,
Georgius Sanctus,

Saviour of sacrificed
Maiden and Princess,
Shelter us and redress
(Georgius Sanctus)

Wrong, the poisonous Serpent;
Return and defend us,
Georgius Sanctus.

HYMN

(For Count Zinzendorf, 1700-1760)

Of unguent in a jar,
We may ensample myrrh;

So were His fragrance stored,
Sealed up, compact, secure,

In flawless alabaster,
But for the spear;

This is the wound of grace,
This is the nesting-place

Of the white dove,
This is the wound of love;

The spear opened for us
The rose of purple fire,

The rose of iciest breath,
White rose of death;

The spear opened for us
The narrow way

Into the dust,
To the eternal day.

SCRIBE

Wildly dissimilar
yet actuated by the same fear,
the hippopotamus and the wild-deer
hide by the same river.

Strangely disparate
yet compelled by the same hunger,
the cobra and the turtle-dove
meet in the palm-grove.

From THE WALLS DO NOT FALL

1944

1.

Wartime England

An incident here and there,
and rails gone (for guns)
from your (and my) old town square:

mist and mist-grey, no colour,
Colorful Egyptian paintings still the Luxor bee, chick and hare *town in upper Egypt*
pursue unalterable purpose

in green, rose-red, lapis;
they continue to prophesy
from the stone papyrus:

there, as here, ruin opens   *modern cf. ancient*
London   *Egypt*
the tomb, the temple; enter,
there as here, there are no doors:

the shrine lies open to the sky,
the rain falls, here, there
sand drifts; eternity endures:

ruin everywhere, yet as the fallen roof
leaves the sealed room
open to the air,

so, through our desolation,   *Spirit of man remains*
thoughts stir, inspiration stalks us   *in union with God*
through gloom:

unaware, Spirit announces the Presence;
shivering overtakes us,
as of old, Samuel:

trembling at a known street-corner,
we know not nor are known;
the Pythian pronounces—we pass on

Priestess of Apollo at Delphi

to another cellar, to another sliced wall
where poor utensils show
like rare objects in a museum;

Pompeii has nothing to teach us,
we know crack of volcanic fissure,
slow flow of terrible lava,

pressure on heart, lungs, the brain
about to burst its brittle case
(what the skull can endure!):

Esdras II — re
Christ's second
coming

over us, Apocryphal fire,
under us, the earth sway, dip of a floor,
slope of a pavement

where men roll, drunk
with a new bewilderment,
sorcery, bedevilment:

the bone-frame was made for
no such shock knit within terror,
yet the skeleton stood up to it:

the flesh? it was melted away,
the heart burnt out, dead ember,
tendons, muscles shattered, outer husk dismembered,

yet the frame held:
we passed the flame: we wonder
what saved us? what for?

Ability of wells to withstand bombings — metaphor for strength of men to endure suffering in search for God.

4.

There is a spell, for instance,
in every sea-shell:

continuous, the seathrust
is powerless against coral,

bone, stone, marble
hewn from within by that craftsman,

the shell-fish:
oyster, clam, mollusc

is master-mason planning
the stone marvel:

yet that flabby, amorphous hermit
within, like the planet

senses the finite,
it limits its orbit

of being, its house,
temple, fane, shrine:

it unlocks the portals
at stated intervals:

prompted by hunger,
it opens to the tide-flow:

but infinity? no,
of nothing-too-much:

I sense my own limit,
my shell-jaws snap shut

at invasion of the limitless,
ocean-weight; infinite water

can not crack me, egg in egg-shell;
closed in, complete, immortal

full-circle, I know the pull
of the tide, the lull

as well as the moon;
the octopus-darkness

is powerless against
her cold immortality;

so I in my own way know
that the whale

can not digest me:
be firm in your own small, static, limited

orbit and the shark-jaws
of outer circumstance

will spit you forth:
be indigestible, hard, ungiving,

so that, living within,
you beget, self-out-of-self,

selfless,
that pearl-of-great-price.

5.

When in the company of the gods,
I loved and was loved,

never was my mind stirred
to such rapture,

my heart moved
to such pleasure,

as now, to discover
over Love, a new master:

His, the track in the sand
from a plum-tree in flower

to a half-open hut-door,
(or track would have been,

but wind blows sand-prints from the sand,
whether seen or unseen):

His, the Genius in the jar   *Arabian Nights*
which the Fisherman finds,

He is Mage,
bringing myrrh.

6.

Worm speaks

In me (the worm) clearly
is no righteousness, but this—

persistence; I escaped spider-snare,
bird-claw, scavenger bird-beak,

clung to grass-blade,
the back of a leaf

when storm-wind
tore it from its stem;

I escaped, I explored
rose-thorn forest,

was rain-swept
down the valley of a leaf;

76

was deposited on grass,
where mast by jewelled mast

bore separate ravellings
of encrusted gem-stuff

of the mist
from each banner-staff:

unintimidated by multiplicity
of magnified beauty,

such as your gorgon-great
dull eye can not focus

nor compass, I profit
by every calamity;

I eat my way out of it;
gorged on vine-leaf and mulberry,

parasite, I find nourishment:
when you cry in disgust,

a worm on the leaf,
a worm in the dust,

a worm on the ear-of-wheat,
I am yet unrepentant,

for I know how the Lord God
is about to manifest, when I,

the industrious worm,
spin my own shroud.

8.

So we reveal our status
with twin-horns, disk, erect serpent,

though these or the double-plume or lotus
are, you now tell us, trivial

intellectual adornment;
poets are useless,

more than that,
we, authentic relic,

bearers of the secret wisdom,
living remnant

of the inner band
of the sanctuaries' initiate,

are not only "non-utilitarian,"
we are "pathetic":

this is the new heresy;
but if you do not even understand what words say,

how can you expect to pass judgment
on what words conceal?

yet the ancient rubrics reveal that
we are back at the beginning:

you have a long way to go,
walk carefully, speak politely

to those who have done their worm-cycle, #6
for gods have been smashed before

and idols and their secret is stored
in man's very speech,

in the trivial or
the real dream; insignia

in the heron's crest,
the asp's back,

enigmas, rubrics promise as before,
protection for the scribe;

he takes precedence of the priest,
stands second only to the Pharoah.

Dream

Ra, Osiris, *Amen* appeared
in a spacious, bare meeting-house;

he is the world-father,
father of past aeons,

present and future equally;
beardless, not at all like Jehovah,

he was upright, slender,
impressive as the Memnon monolith,

yet he was not out of place
but perfectly at home

in that eighteenth-century
simplicity and grace;

then I woke with a start
of wonder and asked myself,

but whose eyes are those eyes?
for the eyes (in the cold,

I marvel to remember)
were all one texture,

as if without pupil
or all pupil, dark

yet very clear with amber
shining . . .

O heart, small urn
of porphyry, agate or cornelian,

how imperceptibly the grain fell
between a heart-beat of pleasure

and a heart-beat of pain;
I do not know how it came

nor how long it had lain there,
nor can I say

how it escaped tempest
of passion and malice,

nor why it was not washed away
in flood of sorrow,

or dried up in the bleak drought
of bitter thought.

34.

We have seen how the most amiable,
under physical stress,

become wolves, jackals,
mongrel curs;

we know further that hunger
may make hyenas of the best of us;

let us, therefore (though we do not forget
Love, the Creator,

her chariot and white doves),
entreat Hest,

Aset, Isis, the great enchantress,
in her attribute of Serqet,

Aphrodite (Venus) the original great-mother,
who drove

harnessed scorpions
before her.

36.

In no wise is the pillar-of-fire
that went before

different from the pillar-of-fire
that comes after;

chasm, schism in consciousness
must be bridged over;

we are each, householder,
each with a treasure;

now is the time to re-value
our secret hoard

in the light of both past and future,
for whether

coins, gems, gold
beakers, platters,

or merely
talismans, records or parchments,

explicitly, we are told,
it contains

*for every scribe
which is instructed,*

*things new
and old.*

37.

Thou shalt have none other gods but me;
not on the sea

shall we entreat Triton or Dolphin,
not on the land

shall we lift rapt face and clasp hands
before laurel or oak-tree,

not in the sky
shall we invoke separately

Orion or Sirius
or the followers of the Bear,

not in the higher air
of Algorab, Regulus or Deneb

shall we cry
for help—or shall we?

4.

Not in our time, O Lord,
the plowshare for the sword,

not in our time, the knife,
sated with life-blood and life,

to trim the barren vine;
no grape-leaf for the thorn,

no vine-flower for the crown;
not in our time, O King,

the voice to quell the re-gathering,
thundering storm.

6.

Never in Rome,
so many martyrs fell;

not in Jerusalem,
never in Thebes,

so many stood and watched
chariot-wheels turning,

saw with their very eyes,
the battle of the Titans,

saw Zeus' thunderbolts in action
and how, from giant hands,

the lightning shattered earth
and splintered sky, nor fled

to hide in caves,
but with unbroken will,

with unbowed head, watched
and though unaware, worshipped

and knew not that they worshipped
and that they were

that which they worshipped;
had they known, the fire

of strength, endurance, anger
in their hearts,

was part of that same fire
that in a candle on a candle-stick

or in a star,
is known as one of seven,

is named among the seven Angels,
Uriel.

One of the archangels - in H.D.'s poem, he
governs war. Thus war is part of divine plan
for the universe.

So we hail them together,
one to contrast the other,

two of the seven Spirits,
set before God

as lamps on the high-altar,
for one must inexorably

take fire from the other
as spring from winter,

and surely never, never
was a season more bountiful

than this; never, never
was a season more beautiful, *beauty of the season*

richer in leaf and colour;
tell me, in what other place

will you find the may flowering
mulberry and rose-purple?

tell me, in what other city
will you find the may-tree

so delicate, green-white, opalescent
like our jewel in the crucible?

Invisible, indivisible Spirit,
how is it you come so near,

how is it that we dare
approach the high-altar?

we crossed the charred portico,
passed through a frame—doorless—

entered a shrine; like a ghost,
we entered a house through a wall;

then still not knowing
whether (like the wall)

we were there or not-there,
we saw the tree flowering;

it was an ordinary tree
in an old garden-square.

23.

Actual experience — charred tree blossoming amid rubble of bombed out building

We are part of it;
we admit the transubstantiation,

not God merely in bread
but God in the other-half of the tree

that looked dead—
did I bow my head?

did I weep? my eyes saw,
it was not a dream

yet it was vision,
it was a sign,

it was *the Angel which redeemed me,*
it was the Holy Ghost—

a half-burnt-out apple-tree
blossoming;

this is the flowering of the rood,
this is the flowering of the wood,

where, Annael, we pause to give
thanks that we rise again from death and live.

29.

Venus identified with Mary

We have seen her
the world over,

Our Lady of the Goldfinch,
Our Lady of the Candelabra,

Our Lady of the Pomegranate,
Our Lady of the Chair;

Venice - identified with Venus

we have seen her, an empress,
magnificent in pomp and grace,

and we have seen her
with a single flower

or a cluster of garden-pinks
in a glass beside her;

we have seen her snood
drawn over her hair,

or her face set in profile
with the blue hood and stars;

we have seen her head bowed down
with the weight of a domed crown,

or we have seen her, a wisp of a girl
trapped in a golden halo;

we have seen her with arrow, with doves
and a heart like a valentine;

we have seen her in fine silks imported
from all over the Levant,

and hung with pearls brought
from the city of Constantine;

we have seen her sleeve
of every imaginable shade

of damask and figured brocade;
it is true,

the painters did very well by her;
it is true, they missed never a line

of the suave turn of the head
or subtle shade of lowered eye-lid

or eye-lids half-raised; you find
her everywhere (or did find),

in cathedral, museum, cloister,
at the turn of the palace stair.

30.

We see her hand in her lap,
smoothing the apple-green

or the apple-russet silk;
we see her hand at her throat,

fingering a talisman
brought by a crusader from Jerusalem;

we see her hand unknot a Syrian veil
or lay down a Venetian shawl

on a polished table that reflects
half a miniature broken column;

we see her stare past a mirror
through an open window,

where boat follows slow boat on the lagoon;
there are white flowers on the water.

31.

But none of these, none of these
suggest her as I saw her,

though we approach possibly
something of her cool beneficence

in the gracious friendliness
of the marble sea-maids in Venice,

who climb the altar-stair
at *Santa Maria dei Miracoli,*

or we acclaim her in the name
of another in Vienna,

Maria von dem Schnee,
Our Lady of the Snow.

32.

For I can say truthfully,
her veils were *white as snow,*

*so as no fuller on earth
can white them;* I can say

she looked beautiful, she looked lovely,
she was *clothed with a garment*

down to the foot, but it was not
girt about with a golden girdle,

there was no gold, no colour,
there was no gleam in the stuff

nor shadow of hem or seam,
as it fell to the floor; she bore

none of her usual attributes;
the Child was not with her.

35.

So she must have been pleased with us,
who did not forgo our heritage

at the grave-edge;
she must have been pleased

with the straggling company of the brush and quill
who did not deny their birthright;

she must have been pleased with us,
for she looked so kindly at us

under her drift of veils,
and she carried a book.

36.

Ah (you say), this is Holy Wisdom,
Santa Sophia, the SS of the *Sanctus Spiritus,*

so by facile reasoning, logically
the incarnate symbol of the Holy Ghost;

your Holy Ghost was an apple-tree
smouldering—or rather now bourgeoning

with flowers; the fruit of the Tree?
this is the new Eve who comes

clearly to return, to retrieve
what she lost the race,

given over to sin, to death;
she brings the Book of Life, obviously.

This is a symbol of beauty (you continue),
she is Our Lady universally,

I see her as you project her,
not out of place

flanked by Corinthian capitals,
or in a Coptic nave,

or frozen above the centre door
of a Gothic cathedral;

you have done very well by her
(to repeat your own phrase),

you have carved her tall and unmistakeable,
a hieratic figure, the veiled Goddess,

whether of the seven delights,
whether of the seven spear-points.

38.

O yes—you understand, I say,
this is all most satisfactory,

but she wasn't hieratic, she wasn't frozen,
she wasn't very tall;

she is the Vestal
from the days of Numa,

she carries over the cult
of the *Bona Dea*,

she carries a book but it is not
the tome of the ancient wisdom,

the pages, I imagine, are the blank pages
of the unwritten volume of the new;

all, you say, is implicit,
all that and much more;

but she is not shut up in a cave
like a Sibyl; she is not

imprisoned in leaden bars
in a coloured window;

she is Psyche, the butterfly,
out of the cocoon.

39.

But nearer than Guardian Angel
or good Daemon,

she is the counter-coin-side
of primitive terror;

she is not-fear, she is not-war,
but she is no symbolic figure

of peace, charity, chastity, goodness,
faith, hope, reward;

she is not Justice with eyes
blindfolded like Love's;

I grant you the dove's symbolic purity,
I grant you her face was innocent

and immaculate and her veils
like the Lamb's Bride,

but the Lamb was not with her,
either as Bridegroom or Child;

her attention is undivided,
we are her bridegroom and lamb;

her book is our book; written
or unwritten, its pages will reveal

a tale of a Fisherman,
a tale of a jar or jars,

the same—different—the same attributes,
different yet the same as before.

This is no rune nor symbol,
what I mean is—it is so simple

yet no trick of the pen or brush
could capture that impression;

what I wanted to indicate was
a new phase, a new distinction of colour;

*The thing itself and
not the myth.*

I wanted to say, I did say
there was no sheen, no reflection, *91-2*

no shadow; when I said white, *92-3*
I did not mean sculptor's or painter's white,

nor porcelain; dim-white could
not suggest it, for when

is fresh-fallen snow (or snow
in the act of falling) dim?

yet even now, we stumble, we are lost—
what can we say?

she was not impalpable like a ghost,
she was not awe-inspiring like a Spirit,

she was not even over-whelming
like an Angel.

She carried a book, either to imply
she was one of us, with us,

or to suggest she was satisfied
with our purpose, a tribute to the Angels;

yet though the campanile spoke,
Gabriel, Azrael,

though the campanile answered,
Raphael, Uriel,

though a distant note over-water
chimed *Annael,* and *Michael*

was implicit from the beginning,
another, deep, un-named, resurging bell

answered, sounding through them all:
remember, where there was

no need of the moon to shine . . .
I saw no temple.

42.

Some call that deep-deep bell
Zadkiel, the righteousness of God,

he is regent of Jupiter
or Zeus-pater or Theus-pater,

Theus, God; God-the-father, father-god
or the Angel god-father,

himself, heaven y̲e̲t at home in a star
whose colour is amethyst,

whose candle burns deep-violet
with the others.

43.

And the point in the spectrum
where all lights become one,

is white and white is not no-colour,
as we were told as children,

 but a̲l̲l̲-̲c̲o̲l̲o̲u̲r̲;̲
where the flames mingle

and the wings meet, when we gain
the arc of perfection,

we are satisfied, we are happy,
we begin again;

I, John, saw. I testify
to rainbow feathers, to the span of heaven

and walls of colour,
the colonnades of jasper;

but when the jewel
melts in the crucible,

we find not ashes, not ash-of-rose,
not a tall vase and a staff of lilies,

not *vas spirituale,*
not *rosa mystica* even,

but a cluster of garden-pinks
or a face like a Christmas-rose.

———

This is the flowering of the rod,
this is the flowering of the burnt-out wood,

where, Zadkiel, we pause to give
thanks that we rise again from death and live.

1946

From THE FLOWERING OF THE ROD

3.

In resurrection, there is confusion
if we start to argue; if we stand and stare,

we do not know where to go;
in resurrection, there is simple affirmation,

but do not delay to round up the others,
up and down the street; your going,

in a moment like this, is the best proof
that you know the way;

does the first wild-goose stop to explain
to the others? no—he is off;

they follow or not,
that is their affair;

does the first wild-goose care
whether the others follow or not?

I don't think so—he is so happy to be off—
he knows where he is going;

so we must be drawn or we must fly,
like the snow-geese of the Arctic circle,

to the Carolinas or to Florida,
or like those migratory flocks

who still (they say) hover
over the lost island, <u>Atlantis</u>;

<u>seeking what we once knew</u>, *ancient wisdom*
we know ultimately we will find

<u>happiness</u>; *today shalt thou be* ⎤
with me in Paradise. ⎦

4.

Blue-geese, white-geese, you may say,
yes, I know this duality, this double nostalgia;

I know the insatiable longing
in winter, for palm-shadow

and sand and burnt sea-drift;
but in the summer, as I watch

the wave till its edge of foam
touches the hot sand and instantly

vanishes like snow on the equator,
I would cry out, stay, stay;

then I remember delicate enduring frost
and its mid-winter dawn-pattern;

in the hot noon-sun, I think of the grey
opalescent winter-dawn; as the wave

burns on the shingle, I think,
> you are less beautiful than frost;

but it is also true that I pray,
O, give me burning blue

and brittle burnt sea-weed
above the tide-line,

as I stand, still unsatisfied,
under the long shadow-on-snow of the pine.

5.

Satisfied, unsatisfied,
satiated or numb with hunger,

this is the eternal urge,
this is the despair, the desire to equilibrate

the eternal variant;
you understand that insistent calling,

that demand of a given moment,
the will to enjoy, the will to live,

not merely the will to endure,
the will to flight, the will to achievement,

the will to rest after long flight;
but who knows the desperate urge

of those others—actual or perhaps now
mythical birds—who seek but find no rest

till they drop from the highest point of the spiral
or fall from the innermost centre of the ever-narrowing
        circle?

for they remember, they remember, as they sway and hover,
what once was—they remember, they remember—

they will not swerve—they have known bliss,
the fruit that satisfies—they have come back—

what if the islands are lost? what if the waters
cover the Hesperides? they would rather remember—

remember the golden apple-trees;
O, do not pity them, as you watch them drop one by one,

for they fall exhausted, numb, blind
but in certain ecstasy,

for theirs is the hunger
for Paradise.

6.

So I would rather drown, remembering—
than bask on tropic atolls

in the coral-seas; I would rather drown,
remembering—than rest on pine or fir-branch

where great stars pour down
their generating strength, Arcturus

or the sapphires of the Northern Crown;
I would rather beat in the wind, crying to these others:

yours is the more foolish circling,
yours is the senseless wheeling

round and round—yours has no reason—
I am seeking heaven;

yours has no vision,
I see what is beneath me, what is above me,

what men say is-not—I remember,
I remember, I remember—you have forgot:

you think, even before it is half-over,
that your cycle is at an end,

but you repeat your foolish circling—again, again, again;
again, the steel sharpened on the stone;

again, the pyramid of skulls;   w.w.II
I gave pity to the dead,

O blasphemy, pity is a stone for bread,
only love is holy and love's ecstasy

that turns and turns and turns about one centre,
reckless, regardless, blind to reality,

that knows the Islands of the Blest are there,
for *many waters can not quench love's fire.*

7.

Yet resurrection is a sense of direction,
resurrection is a bee-line,

straight to the horde and plunder,
the treasure, the store-room,

the honeycomb;
resurrection is remuneration,

food, shelter, fragrance
of myrrh and balm.

10.

It is no madness to say
you will fall, you great cities,

(now the cities lie broken);
it is not tragedy, prophecy

from a frozen Priestess,
a lonely Pythoness

who chants, who sings
in broken hexameters,

doom, doom to city-gates,
to rulers, to kingdoms;

it is simple reckoning, algebraic,
it is geometry on the wing,

not patterned, a gentian
in an ice-mirror,

yet it is, if you like, a lily
folded like a pyramid,

a flower-cone,
not a heap of skulls;

it is a lily, if you will,
each petal, a kingdom, an aeon,

and it is the seed of a lily
that having flowered,

will flower again;
it is that smallest grain,

the least of all seeds
that grows branches

where the birds rest;
it is that flowering balm,

it is heal-all,
everlasting;

it is the greatest among herbs
and becometh a tree.

11.

He was the first that flew
(the heavenly pointer)

but not content to leave
the scattered flock,

He journeys back and forth
between the poles of heaven and earth forever;

He was the first to wing
from that sad Tree,

but having flown, the Tree of Life
bears rose from thorn,

and fragrant vine
from barren wood;

Christ

He was the first to say,
not to the chosen few,

his faithful friends,
the wise and good,

but to an outcast and a vagabond,
to-day shalt thou be with me in Paradise.

From GOOD FREND

Blest be ye man y^t spares thes stones.

1.

My fingers knew each syllable,
I sensed the music in the stone,
I knew a rhythm would pass on,
and out of it, if I could stoop
and run my bare palm over it
and touch the letters and the words,
reading the whole as the blind read.

My fingers knew each syllable,
as a lute-player with a lute,
whose hand lies waiting on the frame,
who knows the wires are taut and bright,
who waits a gesture from a throne,
or from a balcony, or down,
among the crowd, from his own lady.

If I could touch the stone, I knew } cf. Jesus and women in
that virtue would go out of it;   } the crowd
I plotted to efface myself,
to steal un-noticed to the rail,
to kneel and touch if but one letter;
I wondered if the script were worn
and dim and old, or if it shone,
with light and shadow on the stone.

But when I stood before the altar,
the stone had vanished as if under
azure and green of deep-sea water,
hyacinth-green and hyacinth-blue;
so once a discus, idly thrown,
had slain the Spring and yet, forever,
that death had blossomed, for the power
of Love transformed Death to a flower.

There were no letters anywhere,
but on each bud, each leaf, each spray,
the words were written that beneath
the laurel, iris, rosemary,
heartsease and every sort of lily,
speak through all flowers eternally,

Blest be ye man—that one who knows,
His heart glows in the growing rose.

6.

Time has an end, they say,
sea-walls are worn away
by wind and the sea-spray,
not the herb,
            rosemary.

Queens have died, I am told,
faded the cloth-of-gold,
no Caesar half so bold,
as the herb,
            rosemary.

Rooted within the grave,
spreading to heaven, save
us by the grace He gave
to the herb,
                rosemary.

7.

What rose of memory,
ros maris,   sea rose
from what sea of bliss!

8.

Full fathom five
                and under
the sea surge
                thunder,
    Rosalind and Rosaline
    with Juliet and Julia
    join hands with Maria,
    Mariana and Marina,
    Katherine and Katherina
    and with many other bright
    spirits;
        Iras,
        Iris,
        Isabel,
    Helen, Helena; Helenus
    with other princes leads the host
    from Arden, Navarre and Illyria,
    Venice, Verona and Sicilia;

knowing these and others well,
seeing these whom I have loved,
hearing these—why did I choose
the invisible, voiceless Claribel?

14.

Claribel

I stand invisible on the water-stair,
nor envy Egypt,
drifting through the lilies;
I may go here or there,
bargain for bracelets on the bridge in Venice,
or buy ripe cherries in Verona's market;

call me most proud who wait
even upon the very outskirts of the crowd,
                    at carnival,
or stand among the strangers at the gate,
                    watching a burial.

15.

H·O·

And then I wondered . . .
when wandering by Avon's water,
who best attended him,
squire and page and jester from Arden,
dim shapes or shapes seen and sensed clearly,
and laughter heard and song and history,
unrolled further into the past,
        unrolled mysteriously
        into the future.

114

And then I wondered . . .
what voice it was from Avallon,
calling that last April,
farewell, farewell,
but only to pain, regret, disaster,
O friend, farewell
is only to fear, despair, torture,
say not farewell,
but hail, Master.
                    Was it Ariel?
                    Was it Claribel?

Ferdinand's sister - Does not appear in The Tempest

Claribel's Way to God

1.

I met a Poor Clare with a chaplet   *a*
of beads who muttered as she went,   *b*
and ran her fingers over it,   *a/*
with much of *ora* and of *ave*.

She called the thing a rosary,   *c*
and when I asked her what she meant, *b*
she said it was for Rose-of-Mary,   *c*
heaven-dowered, heaven-sent.   *b*

I asked the Clare why she was poor,
she said she was Saint Francis' daughter,
and dedicate to poverty,   *c*
obedience and chastity.   *c*

115

There was some music in the thing,
that rattled on now of *pro nobis,*
and Rose-of-Mary minded me
of the *ros maris.*

And so I got a woodcarver,
to hew me out just some such beads,
but mine were made of rosemary,
and fashioned and strung differently.

2.

Friar

I met a friar in a hood,
and asked him who Saint Francis was;
he said, a holy man and good,
he preached to wolves and even men,

he talked and whistled to the birds;
I asked the friar, where and when?
The friar said, Oh that was after
he gave away his cloak and then,

his shoes; I said, but how
could he endure the frost and snow?
The friar said it was no durance,
but joy to do his Lady penance.

I asked, who could this lady be?
The friar said, simplicity
and purity and holy love,
and her sweet name was Poverty.

And of her Lord, Sir, who is he?
The friar said, God and God's Son,
the spoken and the written Word,
these Three . . . but One.

3.

I, too, was Clare but Clare-the-fair,
Claribel, not a Poor Clare,
for I was much too well endowed,
yet ignorant, I would entreat

a learned scholar or a prelate,
to show me what I did not know,
to tell me what I dared not ask
the Poor Clare or the wandering friar.

Prelate

I met a prelate at the gate,
his robe was rich with ornament,
he had a strong body-guard before,
and many servants followed after;

I followed with them to the door;
one with his halberd waited there,
he looked with awe at my attire,
stood at attention when I spoke,

I pray your Lord a word with me;
he bowed before the Queen of Tunis
and said, I'll wait before the dais
and name you to His Holiness.

He must have seen nobility
embroidered on my sleeve, for I
was swiftly ushered through the crowd;
the prelate greeted me—my daughter?

He raised two fingers and I bowed;
I said, I come to ask of God;
he said, ah fair, ah worthy lady,
this passion for philosophy

becomes you well, and many follow
the lure of Rhetoric and I hear
the court is all for argument,
Plato, Plotinus, Origen,

Proclus, Ficinus—I presume
you follow Plato, shun the Stoics?
And, without waiting for an answer,
The Arian heresy creeps back,

look to Jerome and Augustine,
Ambrose and Cyprian when in doubt;
he nodded to the servitor,
he raised two fingers and I bowed.

Prelate thinks only of philosophy (not God) and orthodoxy.
Talks but does not listen

I wandered much in Italy,
to find the answer; in Assisi,
I saw a picture of a poor friar,
Francis himself, the mountain wolf,

the birds in branches in a row;
I saw his sandal and a cloak,
worn and thread-bare that was his;
I begged admission to the Clares,

and a long time, brewed rue and thyme *Works with herbs*
and stuffed rose-petals in tall jars,
and all the jars were marked with names,
Orris, marjaram, jasmine.

I told the Mother, I must leave,
for still my rosary was wrought,
differently from the other Clares,
and strung and fashioned unlike theirs,

for other names and other prayers;
for though I learnt what *ora* meant,
and knew *pro nobis* was for us,
their *aves* were not for my rosemary.

6.

I wandered near, I wandered far,
and met with wondrous courtesy;
they thought me one of them—only
one seemed to stare and wonder.

The others thought that I had lived,
the others thought that I had died,
they never seemed to sense or know
that I was a mere marriage token,

who never had a word to say;
but he, it seemed, regarded me,
as if myself, I were the play,
players and a great company.

He said, *I died, I die again,*
but this time, shrived and satisfied;
I said, wait sir; for I would know,
where you have been, where you will go.

He said, I went to Acre and back,
but now I learn, the screw and wrack
are torturing my brother Templars;
was it for this—the Sepulchre?

Acre – seaport in Palestine, besieged by crusaders in 1191

7.

I was in Venice once again,
where ships were docked and wounded men
lay on their pallets, or on straw,
thrown down before the Ducal Palace

and in Mark's square and Piazetta
and all along the crowded Riva;
under an arch, he lay alone,
like a crusader cut of stone;

a lantern cast its shadow on
the cross, emblazoned on his tunic.
Now it is night again, he said,
come Lady, say what you will say,

are we condemned and damned, we brothers,
we followers of the Holy Cross?
I said, sir, this is rosemary,
I am no priest, a nursing-sister

has little time for argument;
I never followed what they meant
by schism and by heresy,
but this will take your pain away.

8.

I laid the spray upon his tunic,
he said, ah Mary, nay, not Mary,
but Wisdom, the Supernal Light;
the trouvères hid in the aubade, *Lady of troubadors' love songs*

worship of light, the Arabs told
a tale of passion and of beauty,
disguised as Lover and as Lady,
to hide the ineffable Mystery;

in Persia, too, and we of Acre
worshipped the same, pledged to one God;
I said, the Clares were very good,
and gave me this robe for the robe

I laid aside, for though I could
not tell their rosary nor their *aves,*
they praised me much for that I knew
the lore of every plant that grew.

He said, *your robe is very white,*
bend down; he said, *are these the eyes?*
He drew me close, I heard his voice,
but once—this side of Paradise.

9.

Consolamentum here and now,
I heard as my lips touched his brow;
to him alone, I told my secret,
Sir, I am nothing but a name,

Claribel; Brightly-fair, he said,
O clearly beautiful, thou Spirit;
so he alone among them all
knew I was other than I seemed,

nor nursing-sister nor a queen,
and he it was that broke the spell,
for as he said, farewell, farewell,
an echo from across the water,

answered from bell-tower and cathedral;
the lantern flickered and went out,
and yet the buds of the *ros maris*
shone like dew fallen on his cross.

He said, I died, I die again,
but this time shrived and satisfied,
and as the bell from San Giovanni
answered San Marco, the dawn came.

10.

Though still San Marco pealed and rang,
the pavement seemed to melt away,
though still I heard Giovanni answer,
I found I knelt in Avon meadow,
      H. D.
I found I stood by Avon river,
but Ariel was there before;
and as he sang farewell, farewell,
my chaplet told its *ora, ave*

to Ariel's song, *farewell, farewell*
is only to pain, disaster; farewell
is only to fear, despair, torture;
say not farewell, but hail, Master!

And then but one chime pealed so sweetly
I thought it Mary-of-the-Lily,
but it was Avon's Trinity;
and suddenly, I saw it clear,
            Claribel
and suddenly, I saw it fair,
how Love is God, how Love is strong,
when One is Three and Three are One,
the Dream, the Dreamer and the Song.

123

FIRE, FLOOD, AND OLIVE-TREE

1.

Why wait for Death to mow?
why wait for Death to sow

who ? (us) in the ground?

precipitate the event
and in a row plant
almond, olive, apple,

for by these fruits alone
shall (we) be known.

2.

And see the bleak sky
dimmed as in a mirror,
and under-water, furl
your under-nourished limbs
into a lily-shape
held to a lily-centre:

*Become a small lily
bud or a huge
Continent*

O be content;
be small, a lily-bud
or spread at will
your limbs, your feet, your hands,
peninsulas and islands
to your body's continent.

3.

You are even a world,
a planet,
and pass from history
and the day's event
to myth and phantasy,
with the Cloud-man
or the Mer-man or the Angel
who spills rain
and snow and hail.

4.

Thou has been slain
the nightingales wail;
the nightingales cry again
thou hast been slain:

Individual pain, agony, grief

red-coral knows thy pain,
the sponge, dredged from the red-coral reef,
witnessed thy agony
and told thy grief.

5.

O do not grieve

*Violence in the earth — cf. "You are
even a world"*

for a torn earth
barren fields burnt forests

cracked riven volcano-broken
hill-slopes islands shrunken
mountains lost:

O do not grieve:
leave the stricken broken cities,
give over prayer

for earthquake shaken
broken husks of old fair river-ways,
dykes fallen

against fire flood famine,
your prayers your fears are useless,
leave this to us,

do not waste with the fever
of distrust; terror subdued
is yet terror,

terror submerged may yet break
the soul-dykes
flood drown.

SIGIL

Now let the cycle sweep us here and there,
we will not struggle;
somewhere,
under a forest-ledge,
a wild white-pear
will blossom;

somewhere,
under an edge of rock,
a sea will open;
slice of the tide-shelf
will show in coral, yourself,
in conch-shell,
myself;

somewhere,
over a field-hedge,
a wild bird
will lift up wild, wild throat,
and that song, heard,
will stifle out this note.

EPITAPH

So I may say,
"I died of living,
having lived one hour;"

so they may say,
"she died soliciting
illicit fervour;"

so you may say,
"Greek flower; Greek ecstasy
reclaims forever

one who died
following
intricate song's lost measure."